A Spiritual Legacy

FAITH FOR THE NEXT GENERATION

12 Studies for Individuals or Groups

CHUCK & WINNIE CHRISTENSEN

Harold Shaw Publishers • Wheaton, Illinois

ISBN 0-87788-612-1

Edited by Mary Horner Collins
Cover photo © 1997 by Dick Dietrich
Cover design by David LaPlaca

03 02 01 00 99

10 9 8 7 6 5 4 3 2

CONTENTS

INTRODUCTION

In recent years we have lost the final family members of our parents' generation. We are now the "seniors." It is a sobering thought. As we have seen one generation pass, we have also seen a new one come into being in the births of our grandchildren, six of them at last count. What delight they bring. What great hopes we have for their lives.

The going and coming of life cycles have caused us to reflect on what elements of value have been left behind. *What have we received from those who have gone before us?* Neither of us had wealthy parents, so there was little of this world's goods to pass along. What we appreciate most is the spiritual heritage our parents passed on.

Winnie's mother and father were missionaries to China. Their lives exhibited their commitment to God. She remembers her Dad's unflagging faith, his sense of humor, his prayers, and the fact that he really enjoyed God. I (Chuck) remember my mother's kindness and generosity, which were the fruits of her personal relationship with the Lord. With this heritage in mind, we have to ask ourselves now, *What of value are we leaving behind that will outlast the possessions we have?*

As we consider what kind of people we want our children and grandchildren to become, we wonder if it's even possible to pass on *faith*. Teaching biblical truths and knowledge is necessary, and ultimately the younger generation must choose faith for themselves. Yet we also acknowledge that virtues and values are more readily *caught* than *taught*. Passing on a Christian legacy, then, begins with who we are and the ways God is working in our lives. Our parents knew God's Word, they modeled faith for us in difficult times, they showed us how to persevere and forgive, and they pointed us to God. These are some of the values we want to pass on. Of course this guide is not exhaustive, but we hope that it will challenge you to think through more clearly about what you received and what sort of legacy you want to begin, or continue, to build.

The Bible is filled with examples of people who faced the same challenges in life that confront us—poverty, power struggles, dysfunctional families—and yet who chose to trust God. With God's help they were able to break the cycle of being bound by their painful pasts and positively impact their generation as well as future generations. We will look at these people's lives to glean principles for influencing those who come after us. Since this is a topical Bible study, you will be asked to look at many Scriptures related to the persons and events being studied. Approach the challenge with enthusiasm.

Since the first family in the Garden of Eden, each generation has made an impact on the next. We are all products of the past, and we are all influenced by what has preceded us. We can choose to remain mere "descendants" of past generations. Or, we can choose to learn from the past and become vibrant "ancestors" for the next generation. Whether or not you have received a spiritual legacy, be encouraged! It is possible for you, in partnership with the Lord, to build a spiritual legacy to pass on to those whose lives you touch.

Chuck and Winnie Christensen

HOW TO USE THIS STUDYGUIDE

Fisherman studyguides are based on the inductive approach to Bible study. Inductive study is discovery study; we discover what the Bible says as we ask questions about its content and search for answers. This is quite different from the process in which a teacher *tells* a group *about* the Bible and what it means and what to do about it. In inductive study God speaks directly to each of us through his Word.

A group functions best when a leader keeps the discussion on target, but this leader is neither the teacher nor the "answer person." A leader's responsibility is to *ask*—not *tell*. The answers come from the text itself as group members examine, discuss, and think together about the passage.

There are four kinds of questions in each study. The first is an *approach question*. Used before the Bible passage is read, this question breaks the ice and helps you focus on the topic of the Bible study. It begins to reveal where thoughts and feelings need to be transformed by Scripture.

Some of the earlier questions in each study are *observation questions* designed to help you find out basic facts—who, what, where, when, and how.

When you know what the Bible says you need to ask, *What does it mean?* These *interpretation questions* help you to discover the writer's basic message.

Application questions ask, *What does it mean to me?* They challenge you to live out the Scripture's life-transforming message.

Fisherman studyguides provide spaces between questions for jotting down responses and related questions you would like to raise in the group. Each group member should have a copy of the studyguide and may take a turn in leading the group.

A group should use any accurate, modern translation of the Bible such as the *New International Version,* the *New American Standard Bible,* the *Revised Standard Version,* the *New Jerusalem Bible,* or the *Good News Bible.* (Other translations or paraphrases of the Bible may be referred to when additional help is needed.) Bible commentaries should not be brought to a Bible study because they tend to dampen discussion and keep people from thinking for themselves.

SUGGESTIONS FOR GROUP LEADERS

1. Read and study the Bible passage thoroughly beforehand, grasping its themes and applying its teachings for yourself. Pray that the Holy Spirit will "guide you into truth" so that your leadership will guide others.

2. If the studyguide's questions ever seem ambiguous or unnatural to you, rephrase them, feeling free to add others that seem necessary to bring out the meaning of a verse.

3. Begin (and end) the study promptly. Start by asking someone to pray for God's help. Remember, the Holy Spirit is the teacher, not you!

4. Ask for volunteers to read the passages out loud.

5. As you ask the studyguide's questions in sequence, encourage everyone to participate in the discussion. If some are silent, ask, "What do you think, Heather?" or, "Dan, what can you add to that answer?" or suggest, "Let's have an answer from someone who hasn't spoken up yet."

6. If a question comes up that you can't answer, don't be afraid to admit that you're baffled! Assign the topic as a research project for someone to report on next week.

7. Keep the discussion moving and focused. Though tangents will inevitably be introduced, you can bring the discussion back to the topic at hand. Learn to pace the discussion so that you finish a study each session you meet.

8. Don't be afraid of silences: some questions take time to answer and some people need time to gather courage to speak. If silence persists, rephrase your question, but resist the temptation to answer it yourself.

9. If someone comes up with an answer that is clearly illogical or unbiblical, ask him or her for further clarification: "What verse suggests that to you?"

10. Discourage Bible-hopping and overuse of cross-references. Learn all you can from *this* passage, along with a few important references suggested in the studyguide.

11. Some questions are marked with a ♦. This indicates that further information is available in the Leader's Notes at the back of the guide.

12. For further information on getting a new Bible study group started and keeping it functioning effectively, read Gladys Hunt's *You Can Start a Bible Study Group* and *Pilgrims in Progress: Growing through Groups* by Jim and Carol Plueddemann.

SUGGESTIONS FOR GROUP MEMBERS

1. Learn and apply the following ground rules for effective Bible study. (If new members join the group later, review these guidelines with the whole group.)

2. Remember that your goal is to learn all that you can *from the Bible passage being studied.* Let it speak for itself without using Bible commentaries or other Bible passages. There is more than enough in each assigned passage to keep your group productively occupied for one session. Sticking to the passage saves the group from insecurity and confusion.

3. Avoid the temptation to bring up those fascinating tangents that don't really grow out of the passage you are discussing. If the topic is of common interest, you can bring it up later in informal conversation following the study. Meanwhile, help each other stick to the subject!

4. Encourage each other to participate. People remember best what they discover and verbalize for themselves. Some people are naturally shyer than others, or they may be afraid of making a mistake. If your discussion is free and friendly and you show real interest in what other group members think and feel, they will be more likely to speak up. Remember, the more people involved in a discussion, the richer it will be.

5. Guard yourself from answering too many questions or talking too much. Give others a chance to express themselves. If you are one who participates easily, discipline yourself by counting to ten before you open your mouth!

6. Make personal, honest applications and commit yourself to letting God's Word change you.

CHOOSING FAITH FOR THE LONG TERM

Ruth 1; 1 Peter 1:17-21

Our society expends a great deal of time, money, and energy to ensure the physical, mental, and social well-being of children, and rightly so. We tend to think short-term, wanting quick relief and fast results. Yet how much time and care do we give to the long-term goals, such as nurturing the spiritual life of our children, the part of their being that will never die?

God thinks long-term. Building a spiritual heritage for succeeding generations invests in that which is eternal. Our faith in Jesus Christ is a choice that has long-term consequences, and that choice will shape the kind of legacy we leave behind. Let's look now at a family in the Old Testament and see how short-term and long-term choices affected those who followed.

1. Recall a time when someone made an important choice that in turn drastically changed *your* life. What pressures or obstacles did you have to overcome because of it?

Read Ruth 1:1-22.

♦ **2.** What motivated Elimelech to uproot his family and move to a foreign land?

How long do you think Elimelech expected to be in Moab? How long did Naomi stay?

3. Put yourself in Naomi's place. Think of all that happened in these ten years. What might you be feeling or thinking during these traumatic circumstances (verses 1-7)?

♦ **4.** Moab was a traditional enemy of Israel. How would you describe Naomi's relationship with her daughters-in-law, even though they were Moabites (verses 6-10)?

♦ **5.** When Naomi released her daughters-in-law from any obligation to her, for what did she commend them? What was her wish for them (verses 8-9)?

♦ *Indicates further information in Leader's Notes*

6. Apparently in the ten or more years in Moab, Naomi had maintained her own relationship with God. How do we know that (verses 8-9, 16)?

7. What was at the heart of Ruth's declaration of loyalty to Naomi in verses 14-18?

What might Naomi have done to create such a bond with her daughter-in-law?

8. In making her commitment of faith in God and loyalty to Naomi, what was Ruth willing to sacrifice (verses 12-13, 15)?

Contrast her long-term choice with Elimelech's apparent short-term solution to live for a while in Moab.

9. What do you learn from this story about

making difficult decisions?

the sovereignty of God in our lives?

fostering faith through relationships with your children?

Read 1 Peter 1:17-21.

10. How does Peter describe what sort of life was "handed down" to these Christians?

Through whom and with what price have we been redeemed?

11. What do you think might have characterized the "empty way of life" for Ruth (see Ruth 1:15)?

12. What kind of spiritual legacy did Naomi hand down to Ruth and the next generation?

♦ **13.** Why is our choice of faith in Christ important not only for ourselves but also for the next generation in the long term?

BUILDING A SENSE OF WORTH

Genesis 1:26-31; Psalm 139:13-18

When the late Jacqueline Kennedy Onassis' possessions were auctioned in New York, many buyers felt they were purchasing a piece of history. It was their way of connecting with that fabled "Camelot" era. However, a friend of ours, Rick Knox, carries a different view of the Kennedy legacy. He remembers that John Kennedy's formation of the Peace Corps "mobilized a whole generation of Americans to think of service instead of acquisition, to take risks instead of playing it safe, to break out of a provincial outlook to becoming a world citizen."

Kennedy's challenge started Rick on a journey of discovering his identity and purpose in life. He was among the first volunteers to serve in the Peace Corps, which ultimately led him to become a missionary in Africa. God has given us an even greater legacy of value and purpose as his created beings. We are his creative handiwork, created with a purpose. What better thing to pass on than a Christian understanding of our worth as God's children?

1. In what ways have older people communicated to you that your life is significant?

Read Genesis 1:26-31.

♦ **2.** What distinctive qualities do you observe here that contrast humans from animals?

What joint privileges and responsibilities did God give to Adam and Eve?

♦ **3.** We talk about children looking or acting like their parents. In what ways do men and women reflect "the image of God," the One who created them?

What character qualities would exhibit the fact that we are made in the image and likeness of God?

4. According to verse 31, how did God evaluate his creation? How does this make you feel?

◆ **5.** Since all human beings can trace their roots to the Creator God, how does that fact enhance a person's sense of dignity?

Read Psalm 139:13-18.

6. When the psalmist considers the wonders of a new life, whom does he praise? Why?

7. What phrases in these verses show the value God puts on life?

What implications does this have for our lives?

8. What light do the following passages shed on our personal dignity?

Genesis 9:6

Proverbs 14:31

James 3:9-10

9. To whom are we ultimately responsible in our treatment of one another? Why?

10. How does reverence for God as Creator influence your respect for other people in your words and actions?

11. Discuss some ways in which we can teach children to reverence God by knowing their own worth and the personal worth of others (for example, How can we instill self-respect without arrogance? How can we help them treat other people and their property with appropriate respect?).

12. What have you learned about your own worth through this study?

How can you begin to communicate a sense of identity, personal dignity, and purpose to a younger generation?

MODELING MATURE FAITH

1 Samuel 1:1–2:10

As grandparents we delight in watching our grandchildren grow up, developing their skills and personalities. It's natural for children to develop and grow physically, mentally, and emotionally. When kids don't progress normally due to physiological problems or lack of good nourishment, it is always a tragedy.

Just as we are delighted to see children grow in mental and physical ways, so the Lord delights in his children's spiritual development. Just as we are saddened when children cannot mature, so God is saddened when there is no evidence of maturing in the faith of his children. Samuel was an unusual child whose mother had an unusual faith. Though he was placed in a less-than-perfect religious environment, he too chose to follow the Lord and mature in faith.

> **1.** Think of someone whom you would describe as a spiritually mature person. What makes them so? What makes someone seem immature?

Read 1 Samuel 1:1-28.

♦ **2.** Describe some of the dynamics of Hannah's home life.

♦ **3.** What did Elkanah's activity in verses 3 and 21 reveal about his character? Where was his focus in his worship?

4. In light of the pressures at home and the priest Eli's accusation (verses 13-14), how would you describe Hannah's level of maturity, spiritually and emotionally? Why?

5. How did Hannah follow through on her promise to the Lord?

What feelings do you think Hannah might have experienced as she obeyed?

Read 1 Samuel 2:1-10.

♦ **6.** What was Hannah's view of God?

Where do you think she (and Elkanah) may have learned about God in such terms? (See Psalm 78:5-7.)

7. What things in your life have contributed to your view of God?

8. Hannah's son, Samuel, became a godly leader of the next generation. In what ways do you think Samuel benefited from his mother's spiritual strength and his father's faithfulness in worship?

♦ **9.** According to 1 Samuel 3:19-21, what additional resource did Samuel depend on for his spiritual growth?

◆ **10.** What are some of the primary resources we have available for growing in spiritual maturity?

What happens to our relationship with God if we don't utilize these resources?

11. Identify one or two areas in which you want to mature spiritually, in order to be a faithful example (for example, make a plan for personal study of the Scriptures, begin attending worship consistently, relate in more loving ways, etc.). Relate what you are learning to a family member this week.

REVERSING A LEGACY GONE WRONG

Selections from 1 Kings and 2 Chronicles;
Deuteronomy 6:1-9; Psalm 78:3-7

We met Maria (her English name) when she came as a student from mainland China. Her prior schooling had been atheistic, yet she was a vibrant young Christian. As we talked about her past, we discovered that her father is a Christian. Her great-grandfather had apparently been led to Christ by Winnie's father, William Englund, one of the early missionaries to China. Maria's grandfather had been one of Englund's Bible school students and was a pastor who suffered greatly for his faith during the Red Guard revolution.

Maria represents a fourth-generation believer in a country where atheism has prevailed! God's grace penetrates all cultures and family patterns. But what if you only had role models of unbelief and evil? How can you pass on something different? As we see from the example of the kings in Israel's history, God's grace can also break the cycle of unbelief from past generations.

1. How would you describe the religious environment you grew up in—one of belief or disbelief? Explain.

Read 1 Kings 16:25-33; 22:51-53.

After the glorious reign of King Solomon, the nation of Israel divided into two kingdoms. Israel, the northern kingdom, had Samaria as their capital city and suffered the fate of several dynasties and eventual departure from God. Judah, the southern kingdom, possessed the temple in Jerusalem, yet they too were influenced by godless rulers.

◆ **2.** Who was Omri's role model, and what kind of role model was Omri for his son, Ahab?

In what ways did Ahab's son Ahaziah follow in the footsteps of his parents?

3. What kind of spiritual and moral environment were these kings raised in? Was it devoid of all religion?

What implications does this have for our mentoring and/or parenting today?

Read 1 Kings 21:1-16, 25-26 and 2 Chronicles 22:1-4, 10-12.

4. What sort of person was Jezebel?

Describe the impact she had on her marriage and on the nation of Israel.

◆ **5.** It has been said, "The hand that rocks the cradle rules the world." What was Athaliah's influence as a parent? as a grandparent? on the nation of Judah?

Read 2 Chronicles 24:1-4.

6. How did Joash, even as a young boy, break the downward spiral of four generations (Omri, Ahab and Jezebel, Jehoram and Athaliah, Ahaziah) that had preceded him?

Who became his role model?

Read Deuteronomy 6:1-9 and Psalm 78:3-7.

7. For what does the Lord hold each generation responsible in their personal lives? in their homes? to their children?

8. What, according to Deuteronomy 6:5, is the key to establishing a positive role model for future generations?

In what ways would having this solid foundation break negative patterns from the past in your family relationships?

9. Compare and contrast the adult and parental role models exhibited by Omri, Ahab and Jezebel, Athaliah, and Jehoiada with that of the parents described in Deuteronomy 6 and Psalm 78.

10. What can we learn from these kings about how to avoid passing on a legacy of unbelief and sin?

11. Draw or tell your own spiritual "family tree," charting your history of faith. Where have you seen God's hand? Are there negative patterns that need to be broken?

12. If you can, try to name someone who was a positive role model of faith for you. What from his or her life would you like to incorporate into your life and legacy of faith?

PASSING ON FAITH THROUGH THE SCRIPTURES

Hebrews 11:1-3, 6; 2 Timothy 1:1-5, 13-14; 3:14-17

Susanna Wesley bore nineteen children. Only nine children lived to adulthood. She was a devout woman of whom it is told that she set aside two hours of each day for private devotions. She gained privacy by draping a large apron over her head. Her active brood knew this was the time not to disturb their mother as she communed with God. Her husband, an Anglican minister, was often away from home. So Susanna assumed the responsibility of teaching the Scriptures to her children.

Her communication of the gospel ultimately reached well beyond her home. Her greatest recognized legacy was her influence on her two sons, Charles and John Wesley, who were used by God to spark spiritual revival in seventeenth-century England. Through their hymns and sermons, believers today are still benefiting from the legacy of this godly woman.

1. How would you define "faith in God"? In what ways was such faith encouraged and taught in your home when you were growing up, if at all?

Read Hebrews 11:1-3, 6.

◆ **2.** How do these verses define faith? How does this compare with your answer to question 1?

3. What truths about God are mentioned? How can these truths motivate our faith more?

Read 2 Timothy 1:1-5, 13-14; 3:14-17.

◆ **4.** How would you describe Paul's relationship with Timothy (see also 1 Corinthians 4:14-17)?

What can you gather about Timothy's faith from Paul's description?

5. To what responsibilities did Paul call his son in the faith?

◆ **6.** We know that Timothy had a Jewish mother and a Greek father (see Acts 16:1). What else do we learn about Timothy's family here?

How did previous generations apparently influence his faith (1:5; 3:14-15)?

◆ **7.** What action verbs describe Timothy's progress in the faith (3:14-15)?

8. What is Paul's view of the Scriptures?

What does this add to your convictions about studying the Bible?

9. How can you make the study of the Bible an exciting adventure for your children or for other young people you know? Brainstorm some ideas.

10. Look again at 2 Timothy 3:16-17. Reflect on times the Scriptures have shaped your life and how you might use the Bible to shape a young person's experience. Discuss.

My experience when the Bible	Ways to pass it on to my child/other
taught me	
rebuked me	
corrected me	
trained me	

11. For the single parent, or someone whose spouse isn't interested in spiritual realities, how does Timothy's story provide encouragement?

12. In what ways could you become a spiritual parent to someone else?

PROVIDING A MORAL COMPASS

Exodus 20:1-20; Matthew 22:34-40

We live in a spiritually adrift culture. Right and wrong are up to the individual. Even a car's bumper sticker may proclaim, "If it feels good, do it." Such a casual attitude makes it difficult to pass on any objective truth. News commentator Ted Koppel said in an address to a university graduating class, "Moses brought us Ten Commandments, not Ten Suggestions." Commands call for obedience. They are not suggestions to be followed if "we feel like it." God's commandments provide a moral compass to navigate the tricky waters of life. Obedience to God isn't popular, but it provides a foundation for the legacy we pass on to our children as they ride the currents of living.

When God communicated the Ten Commandments to his people, they were given not to stifle their lifestyle but to free them to enjoy life to the full. The same principle of freedom through obedience applies today. We would do well to take it to heart and then pass it on.

1. Describe some of the rules established by your parents to teach you right from wrong. Looking back, did they seem to be for your good, for your parents' peace of mind, or both?

Read Exodus 20:1-20.

♦ **2.** Sometimes rules for living seem to come from cold and uncaring people. In contrast, what gracious act of God preceded the giving of the Ten Commandments (verse 2)?

3. How did God refer to himself in verse 2?

Why is the first commandment in verse 3 of prime importance because of this truth?

4. The second commandment (verses 4-6) warns against idolatry. In our society today, what kind of misrepresentations for God can become idols to us and our children?

5. How serious are the consequences of idolatry?

Conversely, how far-reaching are the benefits of maintaining devotion to the Lord (verse 6; see also Deuteronomy 4:39-40)?

♦ **6.** Note the third commandment in verse 7. In what ways is it possible to misuse the Lord's name?

♦ **7.** What benefits might the fourth commandment provide (verses 8-11)?

What time do you set aside to rest from your ordinary activity to worship God? Why or why not?

8. The fifth commandment in verse 12 offers a promise. (See also Ephesians 6:2-3.) In what specific ways can we give care, honor, and respect to our parents?

How do you think the way we treat our parents will impact our own children or other young people whose lives we touch?

♦ **9.** The next commandments are the "you shall nots" (verses 13-17). List and discuss the *positive* actions that would flow from these negative commands. Some New Testament passages are given for reference.

Negative "you shall not"	Positive "you shall"	
verse 13 _____	_____	Matthew 5:43-44
verse 14 _____	_____	Hebrews 13:4
verse 15 _____	_____	Ephesians 4:28
verse 16 _____	_____	Ephesians 4:25
verse 17 _____	_____	Hebrews 13:5

◆ **10.** According to verse 20, what was one of God's purposes in giving these commandments?

Read Matthew 22:34-40.

11. In Jesus' summary of the commandments, what is the basis and motivation he gives for devotion to God and respect for people?

How can Jesus' words offset a legalistic and rigid approach to law-keeping?

12. How can following these timeless standards benefit parents and mentors personally? How would it benefit our families? society?

Look for creative ways in which you can follow and teach these commandments to someone in the weeks to come.

FOSTERING A HEART OF KINDNESS

1 Samuel 20:1-15, 42; 2 Samuel 9:1-13; 22:1-4, 33-37, 47-51

A recent best-selling book is called *Random Acts of Kindness*. In contrast to the random acts of violence that lead news stories, it is good news that a little book on kindness is making an impression. The apostle Paul encouraged the church at Ephesus to "be kind and compassionate to one another, forgiving each other, just as in Christ God forgave you" (Ephesians 4:32).

It's always easier to return kindness to kind people than to those who are indifferent or even hostile to us. Kindness calls for a decision of the will. Being kind is a Christlike character quality we are to develop and be faithful in passing on, as King David shows us in this study.

1. Describe a time when you perpetrated a "random act of kindness" or when you received an unexpected kindness. How did it make you feel?

Read 1 Samuel 20:1-15, 42.

♦ **2.** Although King Saul had been David's mortal enemy, Saul's son Jonathan had been David's loyal friend. What promise did they make to each other?

3. According to verse 42, what gave weight to their pledges? How far-reaching would their kindness and loyalty be?

Read 2 Samuel 9:1-13.

♦ **4.** After David was firmly established as king in Israel, what concerned him about the descendants of his predecessor, King Saul (verses 1-3)?

Who was the source of David's kindness (verse 3)?

♦ **5.** Despite David's brilliant military victories, Saul had repeatedly tried to kill David (see 1 Samuel 19:1; 20:1). With this in mind, why was David's compassion to Saul's descendants unusual?

6. Describe the extent of David's generosity to Mephibosheth. How did Saul's great-grandson also benefit from David's largess (verses 12-13)?

7. Mephibosheth had been crippled since the age of five and was now a grown man with a son of his own. After all these years, how might David have rationalized about not keeping his promise to Jonathan?

Read 2 Samuel 22:1-4, 33-37, 47-51.

8. From this song of praise, identify the ways David had experienced God's kindness ("covenant loyalty"). List all the terms he uses to describe God and what God had done.

9. According to verse 51, who else would benefit from God's kindness to David?

♦ **10.** In what ways have you experienced God's kindness in your life?

11. We are blessed to be a blessing. How can you be a channel of God's kindness to others? Look for ways that your family or group can do a kindness for someone else this week.

RUNNING WITH PERSEVERANCE

Exodus 1:8-10, 22; 2:1-10; Acts 7:20-38;
Hebrews 11:23-27

William Englund, Winnie's father, demonstrated perseverance throughout his whole life. As a boy growing up on a Minnesota farm, he drove cattle out to pasture in the morning and afternoon. He used the morning hours to study his Bible and would preach to the cows in the afternoon. Then he went to China in 1903 as a missionary. He traveled the countryside on foot, in mule carts, and by bicycle, bus, and train. He faced wars and danger of bandits. He buried his first two wives and an unborn child there. Yet, in over fifty years of service, it never crossed his mind to quit. His goal was to spread the good news of Jesus Christ, and he never gave up. William Englund left us a legacy of persevering and waiting on God's timing.

In a day when we strive for instant results and gratification, it is hard to keep going when life's pressures build. Often it would be easier just to quit. Results are not always immediate. As we wait for Christ's return, he asks us to persevere in following him and to pass on a legacy of faithful endurance to the next generation. "Blessed are all who wait for him!" (Isaiah 30:18).

1. Reflect on your childhood and describe a time when you chose to wait for a delayed reward rather than being immediately gratified. Why was it worth it?

Read Exodus 1:8-10, 22; 2:1-10.

♦ **2.** Think about the circumstances of an enslaved people living under a cruel dictator. Why did Pharaoh feel threatened by the Israelites?

With what kind of creativity did Moses' parents respond to the threat of "ethnic cleansing"?

3. Note the partnership of the family in this story. Miriam was probably about twelve years of age. Why was her action remarkable?

♦ **4.** In what way would the time of waiting and inevitable separation have been a challenge to the faith of Moses' mother, Jochebed (2:2-3, 10)?

♦ **5.** What effect do you think her parents' example of faith and perseverance in these difficult years might have had on young Miriam's life? on Moses' life?

Read Acts 7:20-38.

♦ **6.** What advantages did Moses' adoptive mother provide for him?

7. When Moses tried to force his rescue mission the first time, what happened (verses 23-29)?

8. How long did he have to wait before his mission was reinstated? What made the mission worth the wait and successful the second time (verses 30, 34-36)?

9. Moses lived for 120 years. What was his legacy to future generations in the final forty years of his life (verses 37-38)?

What perspective does this give you when you feel like your life has been put on hold?

Read Hebrews 11:23-27.

10. What major life choices did Moses make? How did he evaluate instant gratification with delayed reward?

11. At forty years of age, Moses ran in fear from Pharaoh. At eighty, he responded differently and was able to persevere in the task God gave him. What made the difference (verses 26-27)?

12. Hebrews 12:1-2 says, "Let us run with perseverance the race marked out for us. Let us fix our eyes
on Jesus." Think about your race. How can looking to
Jesus Christ in faith help you persevere?

13. How can adults better teach young people to persevere in difficult situations? In what ways can their relationship with Christ make a difference?

SHOWING HOW TO FORGIVE

Selections from Genesis 37; 39–50

Sara (not her real name) was a middle child born into a religious family. For some reason, her parents rejected her. From earliest childhood she was kept locked alone in the basement. Sara grew up thinking that she deserved her awful treatment and that she was a terrible person. When she finally went away to a Christian college, she learned about God's love and how to accept the person God had created her to be. It wasn't easy to forgive her parents for what they had done to her. After a long struggle, Sara finally flew home one day to tell her parents, "I forgive you." As far we know they have never asked forgiveness or admitted their wrongdoing. Yet Sara was able to say, "For the first time in years, I felt free." What a legacy Sara has begun for her children!

One of the toughest things to model is forgiveness. How can we help those of the next generation choose the way of forgiveness? Like Sara, Joseph suffered abuse from his family. He also chose to break the cycle of hate and resentment and give the gift of forgiveness. The results were powerful.

1. Describe the freedom you have experienced in forgiving someone, or in being forgiven. Fill in the circumstances.

Read Genesis 37:1-11.

♦ **2.** How would you describe this family? What were some of the dynamics?

3. What particular pressures did young Joseph endure from sibling rivalry, from parental favoritism, and for receiving revelations?

Read Genesis 37:12-36.

4. Considering how his brothers felt about him, what did Joseph's willingness and persistence in finding his brothers reveal about this young man?

♦ **5.** To what further abuse did the brothers subject Joseph (verses 18-28)?

How would you describe the way they treated their father (verses 29-35)?

Read Genesis 39:7-10, 19-23; 40:6-8; 41:37-40, 50-52.

6. What further experiences afflicted Joseph for the next thirteen years of his life because of his brothers' mistreatment?

7. How did Joseph respond to his suffering? Summarize his character growth.

What credit did he give to God in the naming of his children?

Read Genesis 45:1-11; 50:15-21.

*Joseph was restored to leadership under Pharoah.
When the predicted famine spread, Jacob sent his sons
to Egypt to find food. The brothers did not recognize
Joseph, but he recognized them.*

◆ **8.** Although more than twenty years had passed, how
did the brothers still expect Joseph to treat them? Why?

9. The brothers expressed their repentance (50:15-18).
How did Joseph demonstrate his forgiveness in both
word and action (50:19-21)?

10. What might have happened if Joseph had not forgiven? What would he and the brothers have passed on
to their descendants?

♦ **11.** Compare the brothers' perspective with Joseph's (45:3, 5; 50:15-18). What did Joseph recognize?

How can trusting God's sovereignty, even over tragic circumstances, contribute to our ability to forgive?

12. What do you learn from Joseph's example about the power of love and forgiveness? How can you pass that on?

ENCOURAGING A LISTENING HEART

Luke 1:26-56; 2:16-20, 39-52

There were many times we wondered if our kids ever heard a single word we said. Likewise, we remember the frequent times our children complained to us, "You're not listening to me." Listening is an art that has to be developed. It is not a skill people pick up easily, even as adults.

We are bombarded in our culture with a multitude of sounds, voices, noise, fast-moving images, and constant activity. It's hard to be quiet and focus our minds and hearts on what is truly important. Learning to listen to God's voice takes time. We need quietness to reflect on his Word. Jesus' earthly parents, Mary and Joseph, had developed keen spiritual listening skills before Jesus was born, and their practice of reflection continued as Jesus grew. Listening to God is essential for our own spiritual health and essential to communicate to the next generation.

1. How well did you listen to parental instruction as a young person? Give an example of how listening to a parent, a coach, or a teacher helped you to think through an issue.

Read Luke 1:26-38.

♦ **2.** What do you observe about this young girl, Mary? From her actions and words and others' descriptions, what sort of person was she?

♦ **3.** How did Mary react to the startling news that was brought to her?

4. What specific statements did Gabriel tell Mary about the child she would bear (verses 31-33, 35)?

5. Keeping in mind her youth and the enormous responsibility facing her in rearing this special child, what part of the angel's message would be especially reassuring to her?

Read Luke 1:39-56.

6. After she received the news, Mary rushed to visit her cousin Elizabeth, who was also expecting an unusual birth. How would Elizabeth's response be an encouragement to Mary?

◆ **7.** From her prayer song, how would you describe Mary's concept of God? What did she recognize about her own need? about God's working in history? about hope for future generations?

Read Luke 2:16-20, 39-52.

8. Following Jesus' birth, what was the reaction of the people and the shepherds (verses 16-20)?

How did Mary respond to these events (verse 19)?

♦ **9.** What kind of spiritual example did Joseph and Mary set for Jesus (verses 19, 39, 41-42, 51)?

10. Look at the remarkable action of Jesus in the temple at the age of twelve, as well as his response to his parents (verses 46-52). How was he imitating his parents' example?

11. In what ways can taking time for spiritual reflection strengthen us to meet life's demands?

About what matters should we do reflective thinking (see Philippians 4:8-9; Colossians 3:1-2; 4:2; 2 Peter 3:1-2)?

12. Children are often accused of not listening to their parents. In what areas do we, as parents or mentors, need to listen to them?

Think of a way you can encourage a young person to listen and thoughtfully respond to God this week.

TEACHING CONFIDENCE IN CRISES

John 11:1-44; 12:1-7

While driving in the car with three of our grandchildren, I asked them, "What do you appreciate most about your parents?" Brad, the eleven-year-old, replied, "Once, I broke something really valuable. But they didn't go wild and take it out on me. They're pretty loving and forgiving, and they don't give us everything we ask for. Grandparents can spoil kids, but our parents don't spoil us. But I think my mom will spoil *my* children." (He was already thinking in terms of a future heritage!)

Since Brad had experienced the security of his parents' love and limits, he was able to get through that little crisis with confidence. The key to this confidence rested in his relationship to them. Likewise, the key for us in facing tough times lies in our relationship with Jesus Christ. We need to show by example to the next generation that God is totally reliable in any crisis; he doesn't change. This study highlights the ultimate confidence that Jesus' love is sure in life or in death.

1. What have you received from your parents, grand-parents, or someone in a previous generation that equipped you to meet the traumas of life?

Read John 11:1-6, 11-14.

2. What is clearly evident about Jesus' relationship with this family?

In view of that, why would Jesus' delayed response to Martha's request seem puzzling?

3. What long-term purpose did Jesus have in mind for delaying (verses 4, 14)?

How do these verses assure you when you have questions about God's love and care in a difficult time?

Read John 11:17-37.

4. Martha and Mary challenged Jesus with the same statement. What does this reveal about their security in their relationship with him (verses 21, 32)?

In what other ways did Martha express her confidence in Jesus (verses 22-24)?

5. What additional revelation did Jesus give to Martha about himself (verses 25-26)?

Even if Jesus changed nothing in her current circumstances, why could she still be confident in him and in his love?

6. Describe Jesus' encounter with Mary. What strikes you about Jesus' show of emotion?

Read John 11:38-44.

7. How was the ultimate goal expressed by Jesus exhibited by what took place (verses 4, 15, 40-42)?

8. If Jesus had answered the request for Lazarus's healing right away, as Mary and Martha had wished, what might they have missed in their knowledge of him and his love for them?

How would you explain God's ultimate purposes to your child or a young person, who wants action right now for troubles to go away?

Read John 12:1-7.

♦ 9. How did the events of John 11 affect Martha and Lazarus and Mary in their relationship with Jesus? What motivated such sacrificial love as Mary exhibited?

10. In what specific ways can we benefit from the spiritual lessons passed on to us by this family of singles to remain confident in God's love, even when we don't feel he is actively involved in our lives?

11. Discuss some ways you can communicate the certainty of God's love and care to your next generation of children, grandchildren or others.

LIVING COURAGEOUSLY

Daniel 1; 6:1-23

Over forty years ago, Nate Saint and four other missionaries were murdered by Auca Indians in South America. Steve Saint was a young boy when his father was killed. Reflecting on his father's life, he says, "My dad left me a legacy, and the challenge now is for me to pass it on to my children. Dad . . . found identity, purpose, and fulfillment in being obedient to God's call. . . . I suppose he is best known because he died for his faith, but the legacy he left his children was his willingness first to live for his faith."

The biblical characters whose lives we have considered were all real people who took risks and lived out their faith in diverse settings. In this final study, we will see another man who was willing to take risks. As he relied on God, he found the courage to be faithful in some pretty dangerous circumstances. We have the awesome privilege of passing on this challenge to the next generation.

1. Has there been a time in your life when you acted with courage when facing a dangerous situation, a sacrificial choice, or an unknown future? How did the experience affect you?

Read Daniel 1:1-21.

◆ **2.** Describe what was happening in Judah's history at this time. How would these events have affected their homeland? their worship of God? their family life?

◆ **3.** What qualifications did the king specify for those chosen to serve in his government? What did their training program consist of?

◆ **4.** Although he was essentially a hostage in an alien country, how did Daniel demonstrate the courage of his convictions?

Think back to when you were a teenager. How do you think you might have responded in this situation?

5. Since he and his friends were only in their teens at the time, in what ways do you think their behavior reflected the training they must have received at home?

6. How did God honor Daniel and his friends for their faith and courage?

What kind of impact do you think their example may have had on the chief officer during the three years he was in charge?

Read Daniel 6:1-23.

7. This most familiar story of Daniel in the lions' den occurred when he was seventy or eighty years old. What kind of reputation had Daniel built throughout his life?

8. What was behind the plot of the administrators?

Why would praying privately at night have compromised Daniel's integrity?

♦ **9.** How do you think Daniel's prayer life enhanced his courage?

10. When the conspirators brought to the king their charge against Daniel, what did the king's reaction reveal about his regard for Daniel? What did he respect most highly about Daniel?

11. Write down and discuss some real situations in the lives of your children or other young people that will require their taking a courageous stand. From Daniel's example, brainstorm some ways in which you can communicate to young people about

having the courage to live by convictions.

respecting authority.

using diplomacy and creative alternatives rather than demanding or rebelling.

trusting the power of prayer.

12. As we close this study, in what areas do you need to grow spiritually? What are the things of lasting value you want to leave for those who come after you?

Pray together for wisdom and courage as you take up the challenge of living with eternal values in mind and passing those values on.

LEADER'S NOTES

■ Study 1/Choosing Faith for the Long Term

Question 2. The setting of the book of Ruth occurs in the period of the judges which followed the conquest of the land of Canaan under Joshua. The people of God were living under a theocracy, that is, God was the ruler. God appointed judges to lead the people (Judges 2:18). This four-hundred year period is generally described as a period of trouble and deliverance. Judges 21:25 provides a summary statement of Israel's spiritual condition at this time: "Everyone did as he saw fit." In contrast, the book of Ruth describes some people who earnestly sought God and lived for his glory.

Elimelech's motivation to move may have been because of the health of his sons as well as the famine. His son's name *Mahlon* means "weakling" or "sickly," and *Kilion* means "pining." Elimelech apparently hoped that the stress of the famine would be only for a while.

Question 4. Moab was the nation east of the Dead Sea and a long-time enemy of Israel. It was a country of idolaters and had a history of seducing Israel into the worship of Baal (Numbers 25:1-3). Because Moab did not help the people of Israel with food and water on their journey from Egypt to Canaan, God had said that no Moabite was to be incorporated into Israel to "the tenth generation," which implied forever (Deuteronomy 23:3-6). Ruth was obviously an exception to this rule.

Question 5. The word *kindness* in Hebrew means "covenant loyalty." These women took their obligation to their husbands and mother-in-law seriously.

Question 13. Be sure and discuss this question in your group, for it is the foundation of our spiritual legacy. Every choice we make is important, and the most important choice we can make in life has long-term, eternal consequences: "Will I trust Jesus Christ or not?" Choosing a relationship with Christ establishes the foundation for all the other choices we make in life.

▉ Study 2/Building a Sense of Worth

Question 2. The Creation in the Garden of Eden provides the setting for our roots as human beings. We are made in God's image and thus are set apart from the rest of creation. We also have different responsibilities toward creation (Genesis 1:28).

Question 3. "God is Spirit; the human soul is a spirit. The essential attributes of a spirit are reason, conscience, and will. A spirit is a rational, moral, and therefore also a free agent. In making man after his own image, therefore, God endowed him with those attributes which belong to his own nature as a spirit" (Charles Hodge, *Systematic Theology,* vol. II, pp. 96–97. Grand Rapids: Eerdmans, 1952).

Question 5. As one little boy thought about being created by God, he concluded, "God don't make junk!" Everyone's roots go back to the Creator and to Creation whether he or she recognizes it or not. We are all connected with this remarkable event in history. Discovering that each person has been handcrafted by God builds personal dignity (we have intrinsic value, no matter what others think of us) and also gives meaning and purpose to a person's life (see Ephesians 2:10). "Great is the Lord and most worthy of praise; his greatness no one can fathom. One generation will commend your works to another; they will tell of your mighty acts" (Psalm 145:3-4).

▓ Study 3/Modeling Mature Faith

Question 2. Hannah lived during the period of the judges. During this period, the tabernacle, the tent of God, was located in Shiloh, a city in the center of the country, and people came there to worship. The ark of God rested there, and there the priesthood functioned for God. Yet even this center of worship reflected the corruption of the times (1 Samuel 2:12-25). Hannah's story reveals that it is possible to live a godly life in a godless culture, to mature in faith, and to motivate children to follow the Lord even when their peers are not.

The question of polygamy may come up. Polygamy was not part of God's original design for marriage (Genesis 2:24), and the Bible shows the problems it causes. But in many Old Testament cultures it was an accepted practice. This may have happened because of the people's departure from God over the years and their hardness of heart, as well as a cultural need to ensure the birth of an heir. Women were valued for their childbearing abilities, and barrenness was shameful.

Question 3. First Samuel 1:3 is the first time that the designation for God as "the Lord Almighty" is used in the Bible. Hannah addresses him this way again in verse 11. The name implies that

God exercises sovereignty over all the powers on earth and in the universe.

Question 6. Education for Jewish children was the mother's responsibility in the early years. She continued teaching the girls domestic duties as they grew older. Fathers taught their sons a trade and also the Hebrew Law before they went on to study formally with teachers.

Question 9. Samuel probably grew in his knowledge through reading the scrolls of the Law in the tabernacle and through personal prayer and communion with God. When compared to Samuel's time, each of us has an unusual resource with the whole Bible, the completed revelation of God, in our hands to study and meditate on.

Question 10. Peter tells us, "His divine power has given us everything we need for life and godliness through our knowledge of him who called us by his own glory and goodness" (2 Peter 1:3). Also read Hebrews 5:11-14, James 1:22-25, and 1 Peter 2:2-3 for some of God's instructions for vigorous growth. Our job is to make use of God's resources. We will never mature with closed Bibles. Growing through the Word gives spiritual strength.

▓ Study 4/Reversing a Legacy Gone Wrong

Question 2. Your group may want to refer to the chart below, which presents an abbreviated outline of the first kings of Israel and Judah. Omri, Ahab, Jezebel, and Ahaziah were prominent as leaders of Israel, the northern kingdom. When Athaliah married the king of Judah, she carried her evil influence into the southern kingdom. (She had a brother named Ahaziah and named her own son Ahaziah.) Not all the kings are listed here, only those studied in this lesson.

Genealogy of the Kings

Kings of Israel, Northern Kingdom	Kings of Judah, Southern Kingdom
Jeroboam (930–910 B.C.) | Omri (880–874) | Ahab + Jezebel (874–853) ┌───┘ Ahaziah (853–852) Athaliah . . . . . . (Athaliah's brother)	Rehoboam (930–913 B.C.) Jehoshaphat (870–848) | . . Jehoram (848–841) ┌────┴────┐ Ahaziah (841) (Jehosheba + Jehoiada) (Athaliah's son) | [Athaliah (841–835)] | Joash (835–796)

Question 5. Note that Athaliah was the daughter of Ahab and Jezebel in Israel. She then married Jehoram, the king of Judah.

◼ Study 5/Passing On Faith through the Scriptures

Question 2. Faith requires an object. Faith in God represents an act of the will that recognizes God as Creator and a rewarder of those who seek him. It is enlarged by trust in Jesus Christ, the Son of God, as the Lord who died for our sins and was raised from the dead. Jesus said, "Trust in God; trust also in me" (John 14:1).

Question 4. The church that began in Jerusalem soon spread to other parts of the Roman Empire. The apostle Paul became a Christian missionary throughout the Near East. On a visit to Derby and Lystra (cities in what is now called Turkey) he encountered this young man Timothy, who would later become a church leader and Paul's associate. Paul obviously looked at Timothy as his son and he took up the role of spiritual mentor in Timothy's life.

Question 6. Although Timothy's father had a different ethnic background from his mother, Eunice, apparently his father was also not a believer.

Question 7. The phrase *from infancy* in 2 Timothy 3:15 implies that his mother and grandmother must have told him Old Testament stories and possibly the events in Jesus' life while Timothy was very young. But the main emphasis is on the teaching of the Scriptures.

■ Study 6/Providing a Moral Compass

Question 2. The title "Ten Commandments" comes from Exodus 34:28 and Deuteronomy 4:13. God had granted a great deliverance to the people of Israel from four hundred years of slavery in Egypt. In the Old Testament when God drew attention to his act of delivering people, he was emphasizing his love and power. God was building a nation that needed laws to guide their conduct. The Ten Commandments given at Mount Sinai, along with the ceremonial law, were the basis for the Old Covenant. In it God called his people to loyally obey him, and their obedience would demonstrate the glory of God. (In the New Testament the act of God's love and power is seen in the death and resurrection of Jesus Christ.)

Question 6. See Leviticus 19:12 and Matthew 5:34-37, emphasizing the seriousness of misusing the name of the Lord, such as a common epithet in our day, "Oh, my God."

Question 7. "The Hebrew people observed the Sabbath by resting from ordinary labor. Every Israelite, with his slaves and even his animals, was to refrain from work so that all might 'be refreshed' (Exodus 23:10-12). God cared for the physical as well as the spiritual state of his people" (Lawrence O. Richards, ed., *The Revell Bible Dictionary,* p. 879. Old Tappan, N.J.: Revell, 1990).

The Sabbath "was given to Israel as the distinctive mark of their covenant relationship with God under law. Present-day Christians are not under the law of Moses as a basis of covenant relationship with God, though they are under the law of Christ (1 Cor. 9.21; Gal. 6:2). . . . There is no instruction in the New Testament to observe the Sabbath day" (Robert J. Little, "Here's Your Answer" in *Moody Monthly,* p. 25. Chicago: Moody Press, 1967).

Question 9. Commandments six to ten might be positively stated this way: 6) Honor human life. 7) Keep your marital vows. 8) Respect property rights. 9) Honor and tell the truth. 10) Be thankful and satisfied with what you have.

Question 10. See Deuteronomy 5:32–6:2; Romans 3:20-24; and Galatians 3:24-25 for additional purposes of the law. The recognition of sin against God is designed to lead us to faith in Christ. The law reveals God's holiness and our sinfulness, and it calls us to repentance and faith. Keeping the law does not bring salvation; only faith in Christ makes us right with God. Then Christ empowers us to live by his standards. Keeping his commands establishes important and necessary societal boundaries. Love, of course, tempers the tendency toward legalism.

■ Study 7/Fostering a Heart of Kindness

Question 2. The word *kindness* here is from the Hebrew word *hesed*, which means "covenant loyalty."

Question 4. David had successfully risen to the position of king over the Hebrew people, and many evidences pointed to a successful reign. In this story, David goes against convention and remembers his friend Jonathan (King Saul's son), honoring their friendship with kindness toward his descendants.

Question 5. In David's day, kings often would solidify their power base by destroying the previous dynasty.

Question 10. There are countless spiritual and physical kindnesses God has shown to us—forgiveness, salvation, grace upon grace. It is also the kindness of God that convicts us and leads us to repentance (Romans 2:4). Encourage your group to come up with a long list!

■ Study 8/Running with Perseverance

Question 2. The descendants of Abraham's family became a nation over a span of four hundred years. During that time the nation had been subjected to slavery in Egypt. This study describes the movement of God to bring his people out of bondage and eventually out of Egypt, plus the waiting, trusting, and persevering the people had to do.

Question 4. We discover Moses' mother's name, Jochebed, in Numbers 26:59.

Question 5. In Exodus 15:20-21 we see a glimpse of the future role Miriam played in Israel. Moses, too, displayed remarkable faith as leader of the Israelites.

Question 6. Before Moses received the training of Egypt, he must have been well taught by his mother at home. This is inferred by the fact that as an adult he had a clear knowledge of who he was and a sense of mission. (See Moses' own words in Deuteronomy 6:4-9.)

■ Study 9/Showing How to Forgive

Question 2. Jacob, the grandson of Abraham, had twelve sons, who became the heads of the twelve tribes of Israel. There was obviously competition and jealousy among these brothers. The migration of Jacob's family to Egypt because of famine in Canaan became the introduction of his descendants to that land, where they eventually became slaves.

Question 5. Not only did the brothers mistreat Joseph, but they showed a lack of respect for their father. Only Reuben was concerned about his father's feelings. These brothers maintained a conspiracy of silence for over twenty years to cover their guilt.

Question 8. Bitterness and resentment feed on themselves and result in self-destruction as well as harm to others. Joseph's brothers carried an enormous weight of guilt for decades. Joseph had already forgiven them. They had to receive his forgiveness and learn to forgive themselves. Sometimes that is the most difficult thing to do. First John 1:9 is the key. Forgiveness, both given and received, becomes a powerful tool for reconciliation.

Question 11. See also Romans 8:28; 12:19-21; and 1 Corinthians 13:4-7 for some New Testament perspectives on God's sovereignty, revenge, and the power of love.

■ Study 10/ Encouraging a Listening Heart

Question 2. Encourage the group to come up with as many adjectives as possible. Most likely, Mary was a young teenager, bright and thoughtful, probably poor, trusting, humble. She depended on others for support, was in favor with God, and was blessed. Jesus was born into an ordinary family, although both his mother Mary, and foster father, Joseph, must have been unusual people of faith. Matthew 1 and Luke 1–2 give clear pictures of this couple who was selected by God to be the earthly parents of the Lord Jesus Christ.

Question 3. In the original language, the word *wonder* in Luke 1:29 can mean "to ponder, consider, or to reason."

Question 7. Mary's song, known as the Magnificat, was a lengthy prayer of worship and praise. After the monumental news Mary had received, her visit with Elizabeth gave her time to reflect on what she had learned God was doing and to remember that he was with her.

Question 9. Mary and Joseph modeled obedience to God (see Matthew 1:24; Luke 1:38), a reflective and worshipful faith, a willingness to listen to God, and the strength to *believe and follow God against all the odds.* Think about how Mary and Joseph's history of listening to God's messages and seeing God's miracles in their lives would set the tone for their worldview as well as how they parented.

■ Study 11/Teaching Confidence in Crises

Question 9. John 3:16 and Romans 5:8 describe the sacrificial love of God and Christ. Jesus said that Mary honored his coming death with this anointing.

■ Study 12/Living Courageously

Question 2. The nation of Judah failed miserably in their obedience and loyalty to God. As a result of their rebellion, God permitted the pagan nation of Babylon to conquer and destroy the city of Jerusalem and the temple, which had been built for worship (see 2 Kings 23:36–24:17). The invading army took back to Babylon some of the citizens, including several of the nobility.

Question 3. The candidates were renamed. *Daniel* means "God is (my) Judge," *Hananiah* means "the Lord (Yahweh) shows grace," *Mishael* means "Who is what God is?" and *Azariah* means "The Lord (Yahweh) helps." Their Hebrew names related them to the God of Israel. Their new names made reference to the pagan deities of Babylon.

Question 4. God had given the Jews instructions for eating for the purpose of health and purity. Daniel resolved not to be contaminated by foods that were considered unclean (see Leviticus 11, especially verses 43-47) or that may have been offered to idols.

Question 9. Daniel was known as a man of prayer. He relied on God. Daniel also knew the Scriptures (Daniel 9:2). We still need both resources to face pressures today. God's work and prayer gave Daniel courage.

Daniel's prayer in Daniel 9:1-19 connected him with Solomon's prayer made centuries earlier for exiled people (1 Kings 8:48-53). We don't know how prayers for us in the past have affected our lives today. Nor should we underestimate the value of our prayers for future generations. "The people who know their God will display strength and take action" (Daniel 11:32, NASB).

WHAT SHOULD WE STUDY NEXT?

To help your group answer that question, we've listed the Fisherman Guides by category so you can choose your next study.

TOPICAL STUDIES

Angels, Wright
Becoming Women of Purpose, Barton
Building Your House on the Lord, Brestin
The Creative Heart of God, Goring
Discipleship, Reapsome
Doing Justice, Showing Mercy, Wright
Encouraging Others, Johnson
The End Times, Rusten
Examining the Claims of Jesus, Brestin
Friendship, Brestin
The Fruit of the Spirit, Briscoe
Great Doctrines of the Bible, Board
Great Passages of the Bible, Plueddemann
Great Prayers of the Bible, Plueddemann
Growing Through Life's Challenges, Reapsome
Guidance & God's Will, Stark
Heart Renewal, Goring
Higher Ground, Brestin

Integrity, Engstrom & Larson
Lifestyle Priorities, White
Marriage, Stevens
Miracles, Castleman
One Body, One Spirit, Larson
The Parables of Jesus, Hunt
Prayer, Jones
The Prophets, Wright
Proverbs & Parables, Brestin
Satisfying Work, Stevens & Schoberg
Senior Saints, Reapsome
Sermon on the Mount, Hunt
A Spiritual Legacy, Christensen
Spiritual Warfare, Moreau
The Ten Commandments, Briscoe
Who Is God? Seemuth
Who Is Jesus? Van Reken
Who Is the Holy Spirit? Knuckles & Van Reken
Wisdom for Today's Woman: Insights from Esther, Smith
Witnesses to All the World, Plueddemann
Worship, Sibley

BIBLE BOOK STUDIES

Genesis, Fromer & Keyes

Exodus, Larsen

Job, Klug

Psalms, Klug

Proverbs: Wisdom That Works, Wright

Jeremiah, Reapsome

Jonah, Habakkuk, & Malachi, Fromer & Keyes

Matthew, Sibley

Mark, Christensen

Luke, Keyes

John: Living Word, Kuniholm

Acts 1-12, Christensen

Paul (Acts 13-28), Christiansen

Romans: The Christian Story, Reapsome

1 Corinthians, Hummel

Strengthened to Serve (2 Corinthians), Plueddemann

Galatians, Titus & Philemon, Kuniholm

Ephesians, Baylis

Philippians, Klug

Colossians, Shaw

Letters to the Thessalonians, Fromer & Keyes

Letters to Timothy, Fromer & Keyes

Hebrews, Hunt

James, Christensen

1 & 2 Peter, Jude, Brestin

How Should a Christian Live? (1, 2 & 3 John), Brestin

Revelation, Hunt

BIBLE CHARACTER STUDIES

David: Man after God's Own Heart, Castleman

Elijah, Castleman

Great People of the Bible, Plueddemann

King David: Trusting God for a Lifetime, Castleman

Men Like Us, Heidebrecht & Scheuermann

Moses, Asimakoupoulos

Paul (Acts 13-28), Christensen

Ruth & Daniel, Stokes

Women Like Us, Barton

Women Who Achieved for God, Christensen

Women Who Believed God, Christensen